ADULT COLORING BOOK

MANDALA

Flowers and Doodles Patterns Designs

TEST YOUR COLOR

TEST YOUR COLOR

1.

www.ingramcontent.com/pod-product-compliance
Lightning Source LLC
Chambersburg PA
CBHW081412280526
45788CB00009B/3076
* 9 7 8 1 5 4 4 9 3 3 0 8 5 *